THE BIG GREEN BEAN

by Marcia Wiesbauer

illustrated by Trina Schart Hyman

SILVER PRESS

Parsippany, New Jersey

Published by Silver Press, an imprint of Silver Burdett Press,
A Paramount Communications Company, 299 Jefferson Road, Parsippany, NJ 07054
Printed in Mexico
10 9 8 7 6 5 4 3 2 1

Library of Congress Cataloging-in-Publication Data
Wiesbauer, Marcia.
The big green bean/by Marcia Wiesbauer; illustrated by Trina Schart Hyman. p. cm.
Summary: When their garden produces a huge green bean, an old man and his wife
take it to the queen in hopes of gaining a fortune.
[1. Beans—Fiction.] I. Hyman, Trina Schart, ill. II. Title. PZ7.W6359Bj 1995
[E]—dc20   94-20372   CIP   AC

ISBN 0-382-24661-6 (S/C)

5-00 Decker 1.00

Once there was an old man who planted some bean seeds.

Soon the seeds grew into little beanstalks.
Then beans grew on the stalks. When the beans
were ripe and ready to eat, the old man picked
them one by one.

When the old man came to the last stalk, he
was surprised to see a big bean. It was too big
for him to pick so he called for his wife. "Come
here and see this big bean," he said. "Please help
me pick it."

His wife ran from the house to help him. The old man and woman worked and worked. At last they pulled the bean from the stalk.

"A fine bean like this is fit for the queen," said the man to his wife. "Let's take it to the city right now."

"But what will the queen want with this big bean, my dear?" asked the woman.

"Wait and see," said the man. "The queen will like the bean. I can just imagine what she will give us for it. We may well get a bag of gold."

The old man and his wife walked miles and miles with the big green bean. When they got to the city, they went to see the queen.

"My queen," said the old man, "my wife and I have come all the way from the country to give you this."

The queen was surprised to see the bean.
"Well, well, what have we here?" she said. "A big
green bean! How nice of you to think of me."

The queen looked and looked at the bean.
Then she said, "You are a good man. For this
bean, I will give you a fine surprise."

And with that, the queen called to some
men. "Go to the bin and get me what's in it,"
she said.

The man and his wife sat and looked at the
queen. "We can't wait to see the fine surprise,"
the old woman said to the queen.

At last the men came back with the surprise.
It was a big red beet.

"Here," said the queen. "You may take this fine beet home with you. Is that not a big surprise?"

"Oh, yes," the old man said. And he and his
wife thanked the queen.

The old man and woman went back to the
country with the big beet.

"Oh, dear me," said the man's wife. "We will be eating this beet for weeks and weeks."

"Yes, my dear," said the old man, "but just think of the good things that we can do with it."

"A bit of beet with figs,
A bit of beet with jam,
A bit of beet with cake,
And a bit of beet with ham.
We can heat the beet,
Bake the beet,
And can it in a can."

And from that day till now the old man and
his wife have been eating the beet.